D1299752

COUNTRIES  OF THE WORLD

Written and photographed by
Julia Waterlow

Illustrated by Peter Bull

The Bookwright Press
New York · 1992

Titles in this series

Cover *Brazilians enjoying the annual* Carnival *celebrations in Rio de Janeiro.*

Opposite *A market in front of an old Portuguese church in Recife, on the east coast.*

First published in the
United States in 1992 by
The Bookwright Press
387 Park Avenue South
New York, NY 10016

First published in 1992 by
Wayland (Publishers) Ltd
61 Western Road, Hove
East Sussex BN3 1JD, England

© Copyright 1992 Wayland (Publishers) Ltd

Library of Congress Cataloging-in-Publication-Data
Waterlow, Julia.
    Brazil / by Julia Waterlow.
      p. cm.—(Countries of the world)
    Includes bibliographical references (p.   ) and index.
    Summary: Discusses the history, geography, economics, culture, and
daily life of the world's fifth largest country.
    ISBN 0-531-18439-0
    1. Brazil—Juvenile literature. [1. Brazil.] I. Title. *(adult only)*
~~II. Series: Countries of the world (New York, N.Y.)~~
F2508.5.W38   1992   91-48018
981—dc20   CIP
                         AC

Typeset by Dorchester Typesetting Group Ltd
Printed in Italy by G. Canale and C.S.p.A., Turin

Contents

All words that appear in **bold** in the text are explained in the glossary.

1 Introducing Brazil

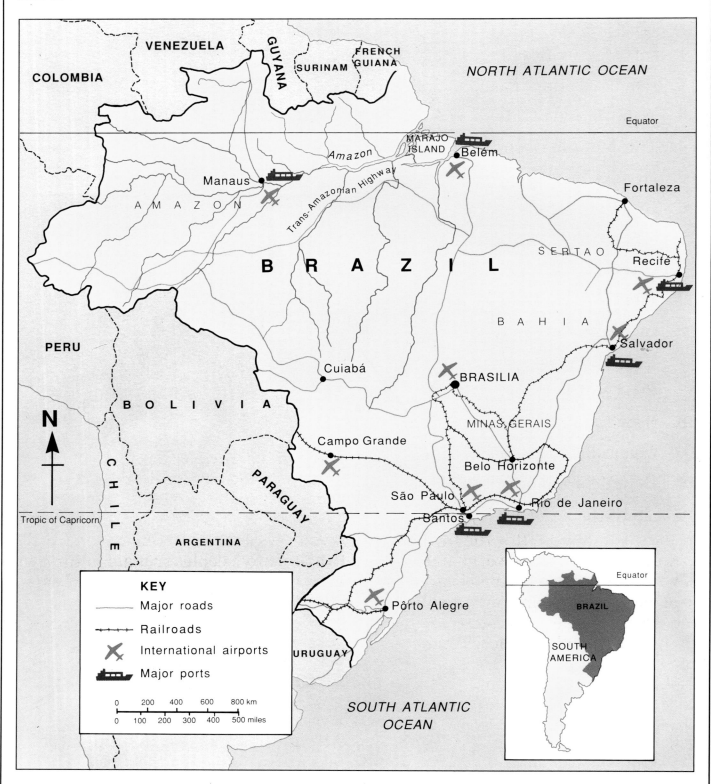

VENEZUELA

GUYANA

SURINAM

FRENCH GUIANA

COLOMBIA

NORTH ATLANTIC OCEAN

Equator

Amazon

MARAJO ISLAND

Belém

Manaus

A M A Z O N

Trans-Amazonian Highway

Fortaleza

B R A Z I L

S E R T A O

Recife

B A H I A

Salvador

PERU

Cuiabá

BRASILIA

BOLIVIA

MINAS GERAIS

N

Campo Grande

Belo Horizonte

CHILE

São Paulo

Rio de Janeiro

Tropic of Capricorn

Santos

PARAGUAY

ARGENTINA

URUGUAY

Pôrto Alegre

KEY

——— Major roads

+++++ Railroads

✕ International airports

🚢 Major ports

| 0 | 200 | 400 | 600 | 800 km |
| 0 | 100 | 200 | 300 | 400 | 500 miles |

SOUTH ATLANTIC OCEAN

Equator

BRAZIL

SOUTH AMERICA

Brazil

Population: 150 million (1991)
Capital city: Brasilia
Land area: 3,286,483 sq mi
Language: Portuguese
Religion: Roman Catholic
Currency: Cruzeiro

Right After school and on weekends Brazil's sandy beaches are crowded with young people.

If you imagine a country larger than all the European countries put together and nearly as big as the United States, then you have an idea of the size of Brazil. It is the fifth largest country in the world and covers half the South American continent. Its borders join it to all the other South American countries except Chile and Ecuador. To the east the coast stretches hundreds of miles along the Atlantic Ocean.

As you might expect in such a vast country, Brazil has many contrasts. The huge Amazon rainforest in the north contains unexplored jungle and is one of the world's last great frontiers. The **Amerindians** of the rainforest still live by hunting and gathering food, as they have for hundreds of years. In the northeast of Brazil many people struggle to survive in a poor and often **drought-ridden** area. The south has rich farmland and industrial cities. Many people here lead modern, comfortable lives.

Brazilians are a colorful mixture of races, a blend of Amerindian, European and African peoples. They have a great love of music, dance and soccer and are, in general, relaxed outgoing people.

2 Land and climate

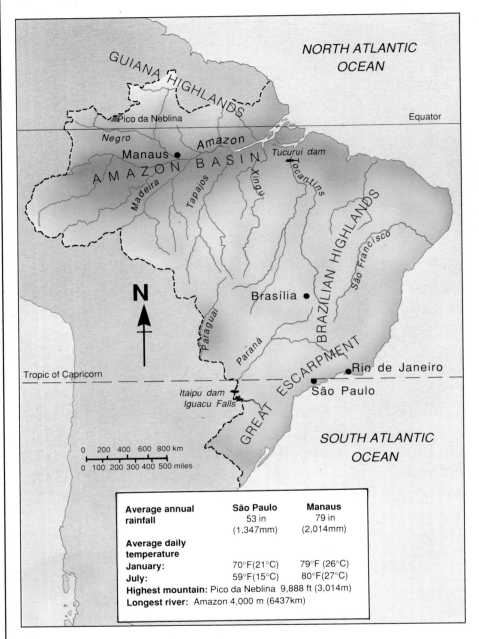

A sugarcane plantation in the south. Red earth and big skies are typical of Brazil.

Average annual rainfall	São Paulo	Manaus
	53 in	79 in
	(1,347mm)	(2,014mm)
Average daily temperature		
January:	70°F(21°C)	79°F (26°C)
July:	59°F(15°C)	80°F(27°C)
Highest mountain: Pico da Neblina 9,888 ft (3,014m)		
Longest river: Amazon 4,000 m (6437km)		

A high range of hills behind the coast discouraged the first white settlers from exploring the interior of Brazil. An **escarpment** that rises as high as 9,500 ft (2,895 m) in the south runs just inland along much of the coast.

Behind this barrier the landscape is like a **tableland** with occasional ripples of hills, sloping gently toward the great Amazon River Basin to the northwest. A large part of the plateau is scrubland of stunted trees and grass.

Almost half the total area of Brazil lies within the Amazon Basin. Much of the Amazon is dense rainforest crossed by rivers. The Paraná and Paraguai rivers in the south of Brazil form another large river basin. In the rainy season the area around the Paraguai River becomes a huge swamp.

The equator passes through the Amazon Basin in the far north of Brazil. The climate here is **equatorial**, hot and wet with little difference between summer and winter. In Manaus, the average annual rainfall is about three times that in San Francisco or London, and the temperature hovers around 80°F (27°C) all year. Much of the rest of Brazil has a warm tropical climate that does not have big seasonal changes. The temperature might drop from a high of 86°F (30°C) in the summer to a low of 59°F (15°C) in the winter. There is usually heavier rain in the summer. Because Brazil lies in the **southern hemisphere**, summer is in December and winter in July.

In the far south and in the hills of the southeast, it can get quite cool in the winter, with frosts and sometimes even snow. In contrast, the large region inland, in the northeast of Brazil, is baking hot all year and often suffers from droughts. Called the *sertao*, it is desert-like, with cactus, thorns and shrubs.

Above One of the highest ranges of mountains in Brazil is the Sierra dos Orgaos ("mountains of the organs"), so-called because the rocks rise up like organ pipes. It lies just inland from Rio de Janeiro.

Left The huge Iguacu Falls on the border with Argentina stretch for several miles.

3 Wildlife and plants

Brazil is a treasure-house of animals, birds, insects and plants; half the **species** in the world live or grow here. Most are found in the Amazon Basin, where new types of plants appear and die all the time. Many have yet to be discovered and studied. However, because large areas of rainforest are being destroyed, some species will never be known about, and others are under threat of **extinction.**

Right A golden lion tamarin. People are trying to save these monkeys from extinction.

Below A jaguar snoozes in the heat. Jaguars are still to be found in the wilds of the Amazon forest.

There are few very big animals in Brazil. Some of the largest are jaguars, tapirs and capybaras. Strange animals include the anteater, with its long thin tongue for collecting ants to eat, the furry sloth that spends all its time hanging upside down in trees, and the armadillo with its shell-like flexible armor. In the forests, too, you can find all kinds of monkeys, insects, butterflies, spiders and snakes. The anaconda, the largest snake in the world, grows up to 40 ft (12 m) in length and can easily swallow a creature the size of a pig.

Above A red, blue and yellow macaw. A macaw is well-adapted to life in the forest; it uses its beak and feet for climbing.

Above A small alligator basks on the rocks. In parts of Brazil alligators are under threat because so many are being killed for their skins.

Below A (dead) piranha *fish. A school of hungry* piranha *can kill a person in seconds.*

Birdlife is exotic and varied. It includes the tiny hummingbird, with its long beak like a spike, designed to collect the nectar from deep-necked flowers, large-billed toucans and bright-plumaged parrots. Apart from alligators that inhabit many rivers, there are thousands of types of fish. The electric eel kills its prey by sending out a powerful electric shock, and the piranha fish tears meat apart using razor-sharp teeth. Gentle fresh-water dolphins enjoy leaping and somersaulting in the rivers of the Amazon.

There are thousands of different trees and plants, some of the best known being hardwood trees, Brazil nut trees, giant water lilies and orchids. Rubber trees and the *sorva* tree produce useful **sap**. The *sorva* sap is used to make chewing-gum.

4 The Amazon Basin

A ferry sets off as the sun sets over the Madeira River, the longest tributary of the Amazon.

The Amazon River rises high up in the Andes, over 4,000 mi (6,400 km) from the Atlantic Ocean. As it flows east it collects water from over a thousand **tributaries**, making it the greatest river system in the world. It is so wide, as it flows through Brazil, that in places it seems like an inland sea. The Amazon Basin contains one-fifth of the world's fresh water.

Much of the basin contains **primary rainforest**. From above it looks like an endless green carpet, disturbed only by silvery snaking rivers. The tops of the trees pack closely together, forming the forest **canopy**, which is full of wildlife such as birds and monkeys. Below the canopy it is dark and gloomy, the tall tree trunks soaring up to 165 ft (50 m), like columns in a cathedral. Few plants thrive here in the dark, but **lianas** and creepers twist around tree trunks.

In 4 sq mi (10 sq km) of Amazon rainforest there can be 750 tree and plant species, 125 **mammal** types, 400 different birds, 100 varieties of reptiles and thousands of species of insects. Besides fruits, rubber and wood, the forest contains many plants that are useful as medicines.

The huge trees in the Amazon forest have thick buttress roots to support them.

A rubber tapper collects the white sap from a rubber tree in the Amazon forest.

Despite its size, the rainforest is a fragile **ecosystem**. Sometimes, if large areas are cleared, rain washes away the soil, turning the land into a kind of desert. Otherwise scrub and small trees appear but it will take hundreds of years, if ever, for the big trees to grow back again. Huge areas of rainforest are being cleared, much of it for cattle farming. Most Amazonian soils are relatively **infertile**, and after a few years crops or grass stop growing well. So the land is abandoned, quite often leaving behind an unusable wasteland.

5 History

During the nineteenth-century Amazonian rubber boom, forest peoples used as "tappers" were treated like slaves.

People have lived in Brazil for thousands of years, but little is known of their history. The first white people to come to Brazil were the Portuguese in 1500. They began to settle and named their new colony Brazil, after a tree they found that gave a red dye called *brasa*.

In the 1500s the Portuguese settlers grew sugarcane along the northeast coast and exported sugar to Europe. At first they forced Amerindians living in the country to work on the plantations, but many died of disease. Over the next two centuries the Portuguese transported millions of **slaves** from Africa to work on their plantations in Brazil.

During this time Portuguese adventurers called *bandeirantes* set off through hostile land to explore the interior and to search for slaves and gold. When gold was discovered in Minas Gerais, in the southeast, many people went to settle in the area, and in 1763 the government was moved from Salvador to Rio de Janeiro. Dom Pedro, the son of the King of Portugal, declared Brazil independent of Portugal in 1822 and made himself emperor. The second emperor, Dom Pedro II, was a respected and good ruler, but his support of the **abolition** of slavery in 1888 angered rich landowners. In 1889 power was taken from him, and a **republic** was declared.

In 1930 a popular dictator called Getulio Vargas came to power. He introduced many social reforms and encouraged new industry. But by 1964 the **economy** was failing and military forces took control of the country. At first the economy improved, but the government was borrowing huge sums of money from foreign banks to pay for big development projects. Brazil was deep in **debt**, **inflation** soared and people wanted a new government. In 1985, after demonstrations and strikes, a **civilian** government came to power.

A view over the old town of Ouro Preto. It was the center of the gold mining region of Minas Gerais in the 1700s.

Important dates

3000 B.C.	People believed to have been living in Brazil.
A.D. 1500	The Portuguese explorer Pedro Alvares Cabral comes to Brazil.
A.D. 1549	Salvador is made the capital and Jesuit missionaries arrive in Brazil.
1600 onward	*Bandeirantes* set out to explore the interior; slaves are brought from Africa.
1630–1654	The Dutch occupy parts of the northeast but are driven out.
1698	Gold first found in Minas Gerais. Wealth begins to shift from the northeast to the southeast.
1763	Rio de Janeiro becomes the capital of Brazil.
1822	Dom Pedro I declares Brazil independent of Portugal.
1840	Dom Pedro II becomes emperor of Brazil.
1864–1870	War with Paraguay.
1888	Abolition of slavery.
1889	Collapse of **monarchy**, Dom Pedro II gives up the throne and Brazil is declared a republic.
1890–1930	Mass immigration from Europe to the Americas.
1930	Getulio Vargas takes power; many economic reforms and progress.
1955–1961	Juscelino Kubitschek elected president and the new capital Brasilia is built.
1964	The military take power.
1985	The military step down and a new civilian government is formed.
1989	Fernando Collor de Mello elected president.

6 Brazilian people

About 150 million people live in Brazil. Like the United States, it is a relatively new nation, made up of people from different parts of the world. Although many are descended from the Portuguese, and the national language is Portuguese, the majority of Brazilians have **ancestors** from other places.

This mixing of races started in the **colonial period**. When they settled in the interior, Portuguese men would often take Amerindian wives. In the northeast there were mixed marriages between African slaves and Portuguese. People with both African and Portuguese blood are called mulattos. Today it is not unusual for a Brazilian to be a mixture of Portuguese, African and Amerindian.

Above This is an area in São Paulo where many Brazilians of Japanese origin live. The stores have signs in Japanese as well as Portuguese.

Left Brazilian children selling snacks on the beach.

This woman and boy are Ukrainians. Their ancestors came from the Ukraine, and the woman still wears the traditional dress of the Ukraine.

By the late 1800s the area around São Paulo had become the great coffee-growing region of Brazil. It soon developed into the industrial heartland of the country. Workers were needed, and several million **immigrants**, including many Italians and Japanese, came to Brazil. Today there are certain districts of São Paulo where you could easily believe you were in Italy or Japan.

The very south of Brazil, too, has many people who are descendants of immigrants who arrived in the late 1800s, such as the farming communities of Germans and Ukrainians. Other European and Asian people – Arabs, Jews and Russians – have also settled in Brazil.

The different races that make up Brazilians have kept many of their own traditions and customs. African music and religion, for example, are still strong influences today. This mixture of traditions means that Brazilian culture is lively and varied and Brazil is one of the more **racially tolerant** countries in the world.

7 The peoples of the Amazon

Above *A young Amerindian girl.*

Left *Amerindians believe in working together and sharing their food. This meat will be shared among several families.*

Before white people came there were probably as many as 5 million Amerindians in Brazil. Thousands died when they were made slaves and when the new settlers took their land. The biggest killers of all have been European diseases such as influenza and smallpox, to which Amerindians have no natural resistance. Today there are fewer than 200,000 Amerindians left in Brazil.

There are many different Amerindian peoples living in the rainforest, and their ways of life vary. However, Amerindians traditionally live by gathering their food and using the plants of the forests to make what they need. Besides fishing and hunting, they clear a small patch of forest for crops. Every few years they move on. The forest grows back because they cut down only a small area. They have no need for clothes; instead they decorate their bodies with paint and wear jewelry of beads and feathers. Amazonian Amerindians believe river and forest spirits guide their lives.

There are still remote villages that preserve these original customs and way of life, but most Amerindians living in the rainforest have had some contact with white people. Many now live in permanent villages, wear clothes and have adopted other ways of modern civilization. Their beliefs and culture have changed as, over the years, **missionaries** have taught them about Christianity.

The Amerindians of the rainforest are under great pressure from outsiders who want their land in order to **exploit** the Amazon's natural resources. The government has set up some reservations where land is set aside solely for the use of these Amerindians. Here they can continue their traditional way of life. However it is difficult to protect the boundaries of these reservations because they are in such remote areas of the Amazon region.

In 1989, more than 500 Amerindians gathered to protest about the government's plans to build dams on their land.

8 Cities

More than two-thirds of the Brazilian people live in towns, and there are many large cities. Most of the cities are in the south and along the east coast. Although Brazilian cities have modern buildings and skyscrapers, they are surrounded by *favelas* (slums). The poor people live here in shacks made from tin and cardboard collected from garbage dumps. They are often without electricity, water or modern toilets.

About 14 million people live in São Paulo, making it the second largest city in the world. It is the commercial and industrial heart of Brazil as well as being a lively center for music and the arts.

Above View across Rio de Janeiro and the famous Sugar Loaf mountain.

Left This square in the center of Rio de Janeiro has black and white paving, typical of Brazilian cities.

Above Favelas *on the outskirts of São Paulo. People leave the poor areas of Brazil and build themselves a house wherever they can find space around the cities.*

Rio de Janeiro, once the capital of Brazil, has one of the most beautiful settings in the world. It lies where hills covered with tropical vegetation meet the sandy beaches of the Atlantic Ocean. Not only is it a fashionable resort, but it is also an important commercial city. The contrast between rich and poor is seen sharply here; above the expensive seaside apartment buildings, shabby *favelas* cling to the hillsides.

In order to open up the interior of Brazil, in 1956 a brand new capital city called Brasilia was planned. The area was so remote and undeveloped that workers, building materials and food all had to be flown in. The city has futuristic buildings lining broad avenues. Brasilia was completed in 1960 and is now the capital.

The cathedral in Brasilia is one of many exciting modern buildings that are to be found in the capital.

In many of the cities in the east you can still see old colonial Portuguese buildings. Manaus, in the middle of the Amazon Basin, has a grand old opera house, which is a reminder of the importance of the city during the Amazonian rubber boom.

9 Family and home

Left *Many of Brazil's cities sprout modern high rise apartment and office buildings. This is Campo Grande, the center of a rich cattle region in the southwest.*

Below *Many homes do not have running water. These people in the Amazon region go to the nearest stream to do their washing.*

The contrast between rich and poor in Brazil is striking. Some Brazilians have money and the choice to do whatever they please, but most people find it hard just to feed and clothe themselves. Wealthier people usually live in a house or an apartment with all the modern luxuries and a car. Many employ maids. For those who are not from a wealthy family, life is very different. In the cities the very poor huddle in cramped shacks in the *favelas*. A family with seven children may live in two or three rooms without running water. Some children in the cities are abandoned by their families and live and sleep on the streets, begging or stealing in order to survive.

Houses in the countryside, too, often have no running water or electricity. Water is brought in tin cans from the nearest stream or spring where people also do their washing. In the Amazon Basin people build simple houses of palm leaves with a mud or wood floor, sometimes on stilts to avoid flood water. Many Brazilians, particularly in the north and in the countryside, sleep in hammocks instead of beds. Hammocks are much cooler and are just as comfortable as a bed. They can also be folded away in the daytime, so there is more room in the house.

Young people usually continue to live at home until they get married because they cannot afford their own place. Grandparents usually stay with the family and help by looking after small children when the parents are working. Big families are common; many people have between five and ten children; some in poor country areas have as many as twenty.

Above *Houses in the dry northeast are often made of adobe and wattle (mud-brick and sticks). In the countryside many people use animals for transportation. This boy uses the family's donkey to carry water from the well.*

Left *Hammocks are common in Brazil, both for sleeping in and, like this family, just for relaxing.*

10 Life in country and city

Early in the morning, some children in São Paulo will be driven to their private school by their parents. At the same time, in the interior of Brazil, other children will be walking barefoot along muddy roads to their wooden schoolhouse. One father will be sitting in his air-conditioned office; another will be hacking at the undergrowth with his **machete**, clearing space to grow food.

People such as the riverside dwellers and settlers in the Amazon region and the interior of Brazil lead simple lives, not unlike the lives of the Amerindians. They grow basic crops, perhaps catching fish or raising a few cattle. Living far from their nearest neighbors, they are very isolated. There is little health care, and many people suffer from **malnutrition** and diseases such as **malaria**.

Above A cowboy in the south of Brazil lassoos a young foal.

Left This family in the Amazon Basin live by a river. The only way they can travel around is by boat.

One of the poorest areas of Brazil is the northeast. Inland, people try to make a living from raising cattle, but with terrible droughts many have given up and set off to start new lives in other areas of Brazil. Families head for the *favelas* of the cities or perhaps for the Amazon Basin, where they can find land for small farms of their own. Apart from living in the large cities like Recife and Salvador, people along the coast of the northeast also live and work on plantations or earn their living by fishing.

In the south there is generally a higher standard of living. The cities here provide more opportunities and there are big mines, cattle ranches, plantations. As in other parts of Brazil, wealthy landowners often own the farms. Workers may be given small houses on the estate and there may be a school for the children.

Above On Sundays, kites are sold out on the grass in the huge open spaces of the capital, Brasilia.

Below Workers on a coffee plantation in the state of São Paulo live in houses like this. There is a school on the plantation for their children.

11 Education and schools

Primary education, called **First Grade**, starts at age 7. It lasts for eight years and is free for everybody. Children who fail to pass exams at the end of the year have to repeat the whole year. **Second Grade**, or secondary school, follows for three years.

Many schools are short of books and equipment, and in poor areas children may receive only two or three hours' schooling a day. Some children have no school at all to go to. Others may have to leave school when still quite young, to help the family by earning money. Many therefore do not have the chance to finish First Grade, let alone go on to Second Grade.

Above A history class in a school on a sugar plantation.

Below These schoolchildren have come to do exercises on the nearest beach.

Many children, like these shoeshine boys, work during the day when they are not at school.

In cities the schools are usually better, and if the family have the money they send their children to private schools, particularly for Second Grade. City children have greater chances to go on to further education and to college.

Most schools teach one age group in the morning and one in the afternoon. If children have morning school it starts early, often at 7:00 A.M. State schools sometimes provide lunch, which is a way of making sure poor children who may not eat well at home at least get one good meal a day. Outside school hours many children go out to work. They start as soon as they are old enough, walking around the streets shining shoes or selling ice-cream, fruit, nuts or snacks. In the country they help their parents on the farm or in the house.

Education in Brazil is important not just for children; more than a third of the population is still **illiterate**. Government programs have been set up to help people of all ages who cannot read and write by providing classes in the evenings after work.

12 Food and drink

Brazil has a huge variety of fresh foods that are used to produce all sorts of regional specialties. There is one dish, usually eaten at Saturday lunchtime, that is the closest Brazil gets to a national favorite: *feijoada*. It is made of smoked meat in a spiced black bean sauce and garnished with slices of orange.

Rice is served with most meals in Brazil. The other **staple** food all over Brazil is *mandioca*. This is a root vegetable, which can be served on its own or, more usually, pounded and dried into a flour called *farinha*. When toasted it is called *farofa*, and Brazilians like to sprinkle it over nearly everything they eat.

A market in the Amazon Basin, with pineapples, Brazil nuts and cocoa pods for sale.

Left Oranges, bananas and two Amazonian fruits – cupuacu (the big brown ones) and pupunha.

Below This woman from Bahia sells typical street snacks found in the northeast of Brazil.

Above The rivers of Brazil have many huge fish, like these on sale in a market.

The most exotic dishes come from Bahia and the northeast, influenced by African cooking. Seafood, chili peppers, a special palm oil called *dende* and coconut are common ingredients. In the cattle country of the south and the interior, dishes such as *churrasco* (charcoal-grilled meat) and *carne do sol* (sun-dried meat) are very popular. Fish is the basis of most meals in the Amazon Basin. Although many Brazilians have some meat, fish or cheese to eat, the very poor often live on a simple diet of rice, black beans and *mandioca*.

All towns have *lanchonettes*, or snackbars, where you can eat tasty pastries and hamburgers, and drink delicious freshly-squeezed fruit drinks. Street-sellers run stands selling snacks like *acaraje*, fried bean cakes with shrimps and hot pepper sauce. Chilled young green coconuts can be bought too – the top is chopped off and you drink the milky juice through a straw. Besides fruit juice and coffee, Brazilians like to drink beer and *cachaca*, a strong spirit made from sugarcane.

13 BRAZIL
Sports and leisure

Left At about 7:00 A.M., before classes start, these children in the Amazon play a game of basketball in the school playground.

Below Every day people come to swim and sunbathe on Ipanema beach in Rio.

Without a doubt the most popular sport in Brazil is soccer. There are nearly always young people outside in the late afternoon playing a game on the nearest patch of ground; if not, it is quite likely they will be inside watching it on television. Brazil has won The World Cup three times and has produced players like Pelé, who was one of the greatest soccer players of all time. All cities have soccer stadiums; Maracana in Rio, which can hold 200,000 people, is the biggest in the world. At matches the Brazilian fans go wild with excitement, cheering, dancing and singing and even letting off fireworks.

Other sports such as volleyball and basketball are played in many schools and clubs or on the sand at the beach.

Brazil's 4,500-mi (7,500-km) coastline, many rivers and warm climate mean that people spend a lot of spare time swimming and lazing by the water. On weekends and holidays the popular beaches around the big cities are crowded with Brazilians of all ages eating, drinking, swimming, surfing and sunbathing.

For wealthier Brazilians, fitness clubs and jogging are fashionable ways of getting exercise. Poorer children and those in remote areas usually play near their houses, perhaps with a toy they have made themselves, like kites, or with something inexpensive like marbles. Men enjoy sitting in the shade of a tree playing a game of dominoes or cards.

One of the most popular ways of spending evenings for many Brazilians is watching television, particularly *novelas* (soap operas). They also love to watch soccer, or their automobile-racing heroes such as Ayrton Senna or Nelson Piquet.

Children of the favelas *just have the small space around their houses to play sports and games.*

14 Music, dance and carnival

Music and dance seem to flow through the veins of Brazilian people. Add to this the many different musical influences from Brazil's different races and the result is a music-loving country with its own special styles.

The best-known Brazilian types of music and dance are *samba* and *lambada*, but there are many others that are just as popular. *Forro* and *frevo*, for example, are favorites in the northeast. On Saturday nights in Rio or Recife, dance halls all over the cities throb to *samba* or *forro*.

Right A band plays at a local gathering.

Below Capoeira *is a special kind of dancing from the northeast. It looks like fighting, though the two people never touch each other.*

Brazilian music like *bossa-nova* developed from *samba* and jazz; Tom Jobin and Joao Gilberto are two of the most famous singer-songwriters. Later, others such as Gilberto Gil and Chico Buarque developed this music, bringing political themes to their songs during the years of military rule in the late 1960s. Besides the nationally-famous musicians, both popular and classical, street singers and dancers are part of Brazilian musical life.

The highlight of the year in Brazil is *Carnival*, a wild celebration of processions, parties, music and dancing. It takes place in the week before Lent. Everything stops for days of festivity in every town and city all over the country. The biggest parades are in Rio, where the *samba* schools compete to be *Carnival* champions. Months are spent making fantastic costumes and huge elaborately decorated floats, and practicing the music and dances. Besides parades, there are costume balls every evening, and people dance the night away out on the streets.

Some of the fantastic and colorful costumes that make Rio's Carnival *parade so spectacular.*

15 Religions and beliefs

Inside Brasilia's modern cathedral.

The Portuguese brought **Roman Catholicism** to Brazil, and it remains the main religion today. There are more Roman Catholics in Brazil than in any other country in the world. Brazilians celebrate all the usual Christian festivals, like Christmas and Easter, as well as many saints' days. At other times of the year people like to make pilgrimages to holy places.

Christian missionaries have had an important impact on Brazil's development, as they traveled far into the interior trying to convert the Amerindian population to Christianity. On one hand their efforts have destroyed old traditions and customs, but on the other hand they have often provided medicines and schooling that these people would not otherwise have had. Both Catholic and Protestant missionaries still work in remote parts of the Amazon Basin and in the *favelas* of the cities.

Although Brazil is a mainly Christian country, Amerindian and African spirit traditions have a strong influence on the people's beliefs. Many Brazilians, both rich and poor, believe in the power of spirits as well as going regularly to church and praying to the Christian God. *Umbanda* and *Candomblé* are two of the **cults** in Brazil that have developed from African religions. Followers hold ritual ceremonies led by a high priestess. She will enter a trance, contact spirits and call on them to help people. These cults also include aspects of the Christian religion; for example, the African goddess of the sea, *Yermanja*, is also called the Virgin Mary. People gather on the beach on New Year's Eve, which is *Yermanja*'s special day. Dressed in white, they throw flowers and gifts in the water to their sea goddess.

Right *These statues in a* Candomblé *temple are called the "Old Black Slaves."* Candomblé *is based on an African religion that was brought to Brazil by African slaves.*

Below *Crowds on the beaches of Salvador celebrating* Yermanja*'s special day.*

16 The Arts

Little is left of ancient Amerindian art, although fine pottery dating back more than a thousand years has been found on Marajo Island at the mouth of the Amazon. Amerindian artistic traditions, such as elaborate body painting, carving and pottery, are still carried on today.

During the colonial period Brazilian art, architecture and sculpture had mainly religious subjects. Many beautiful Portuguese-style churches were built, decorated lavishly with gold and with sculptures. The outstanding Brazilian sculptor of the late eighteenth century was a man called Aleijadinho, who was severely crippled from leprosy. He produced some of the finest sculptures in Brazil.

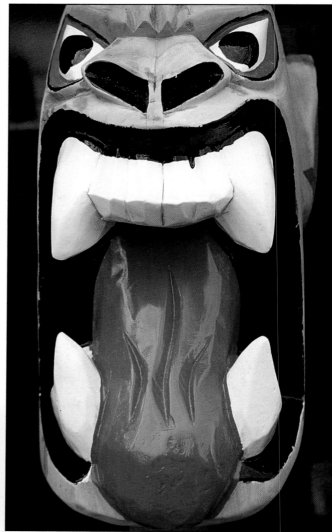

Above Boats on the São Francisco River have wooden figureheads. It is believed they will frighten off evil spirits.

Left A woman works on detailed embroidery. Fine local handicrafts are made all over the country.

Left A painting by the nineteenth-century artist Candido Portinari shows daily life in the northeast of Brazil.

Below "The Warriors," a modern sculpture in a square in front of government buildings in the capital, Brasilia.

After independence from Portugal, a new generation of Brazilian artists such as Candido Portinari and Di Calvacanti came to the forefront. They used strong colors and forms in their paintings, reflecting the tropical sun and intense color of the landscape.

Modern Brazilian architecture is admired worldwide. Many buildings in Brasilia were designed by the architect Oscar Niemeyer. Using concrete and glass, his buildings are fresh, light structures, making use of open space and the bright Brazilian light. Dramatic sculptures by Bruno Giorgi adorn the city too.

Like many Brazilian musicians and artists, large numbers of Brazilian writers come from the northeast. Much of the literature is based on themes from daily life. Books by the famous writer Jorge Amado have been translated into other languages and made into motion pictures.

Artesanato (folk art) is found in many areas of Brazil. You will often see lacemakers, woodcarvers, potters and people selling hand-made jewelry.

17 Farming, fishing, forestry

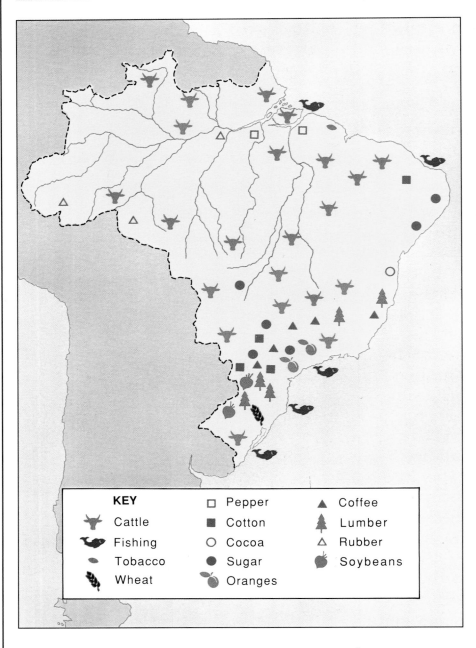

In Brazil much farmwork is still done by hand. This woman is pounding coffee beans in a mortar.

KEY

Cattle	□ Pepper	▲ Coffee
Fishing	■ Cotton	🌲 Lumber
Tobacco	○ Cocoa	△ Rubber
Wheat	● Sugar	Soybeans
	🍊 Oranges	

With Brazil's varied but generally warm climate, a large number of different crops can be grown all the year round. Nearly every fruit you can think of is grown in Brazil – and many others you may never have seen. Brazil is the biggest exporter of oranges in the world, mainly in the form of orange juice. Although coffee is often thought of as the main Brazilian product, nowadays crops such as sugarcane and soybeans are equally important.

Cattle rearing is one of the fastest-growing farming activities. Brazil now has the second largest number of cattle in the world. In the hot tropical areas a special breed of cattle called *zebu*, originally from India, does best. Staple foods like rice and *mandioca* are grown all over Brazil. Corn, cotton and tobacco are other important crops.

One of the problems in Brazil is that most of the land is owned by a few rich landowners. Although there are many small farmers, the amount of land they have is only enough to grow their own food and not enough to grow crops to sell. Except on some big farms that can afford machinery, much of the farmwork is still done by hand.

All along the long Atlantic coast there is a rich catch of fish and shellfish, but Brazil has never developed a big commercial fishing industry. The hardwood trees of the Amazon Basin, too, have not been exploited fully yet – most of Brazil's lumber comes from forests in the far south of Brazil. Rubber tapping was a major activity in the Amazon Basin during the late nineteenth century. However rubber plantations in the Far East proved more successful and the Brazilian market collapsed. Today there is only some small-scale rubber tapping in Brazil.

Fishermen near Fortaleza set out in their boats early in the morning.

18 Industry and resources

Brazil is the leading industrial nation in South America. The main exports used to be raw materials and agricultural products, but industry now accounts for two-thirds of its exports. With its large and growing population, Brazil has a huge home market for what it produces.

Main exports:	Transportation equipment, soybeans, coffee, machinery, shoes, iron ore.
Main imports:	Machinery, transportation equipment, chemicals, oil.

Begun in the 1950s, Brazil's car industry is now one of the largest in the world. Other major industries are the manufacture of aircraft and ships, and iron and steel production. Petrochemicals, textiles and food processing are also important. The majority of manufacturing and processing industries are located in the southeast, especially around São Paulo. One exception to this is Manaus, in the Amazon, which is a **Free Trade Zone**, producing more television and hi-fi sets than any other Brazilian city.

An aluminum processing plant in Minas Gerais.

Brazil has a wealth of mineral resources. Many are already being mined, like the iron ore of Minas Gerais and the huge iron ore mines at Carajas which cover hundreds of square miles. Brazil is the world's second largest producer of iron ore. There also are big reserves of other minerals such as gold, **bauxite**, tin, zinc, manganese and lead. Surveys have shown that many of the untapped mineral reserves lie in the Amazon Basin.

Above Water cascades over the spillway at Itaipu Dam. Itaipu produces more hydroelectric power than any other dam in the world.

Although oil is important as a source of power in Brazil, the country produces comparatively little and most has to be imported from abroad. As a result the Brazilians have had to develop other sources of energy. Because there were so many rivers, they started to build **hydroelectric** projects. Itaipu on the Paraná River and Tucurui in the Amazon Basin are two of the largest hydroelectric dams in the world. Hydroelectricity is fast becoming the major power source in Brazil.

Left Gold-miners called garimpeiros *work the rivers for gold all over Brazil. Stores like this one buy gold from anyone who can find it.*

19 Transportation

Getting around Brazil is not always easy; distances are huge and torrential rains sometimes wash away roads. Although the south of Brazil has a good road network, in the Amazon Basin for much of the year, the only way to travel is by plane or by boat. New roads such as the Trans-Amazonian Highway, over 3,000 mi (5,000 km) long, have opened up parts of the Amazon Basin, but roads here are often impassable.

Above Gas stations in Brazil sell three types of fuel: gasoline, diesel and alcohol (alcool). Many cars run on alcohol made from sugarcane.

Left Boat travel is usually the only way to get around the Amazon region. This is a passenger dock at Manaus.

Above Sometimes buses travel the dirt track roads in the heart of the Amazon Basin. When they reach a river, they have to cross by ferry because there are no bridges.

Right Varig is one of Brazil's four airlines. They have hundreds of routes around Brazil and internationally.

Regional bus services run from city to city. Most people make long trips by bus, some journeys taking days rather than hours. Boat travel is the most common way to get around in the Amazon Basin. For local trips people might use a canoe. For longer trips there are double-decker boats with space to sling hammocks; everyone uses these as transportable beds.

Many Brazilians now own cars, but they do not all run on gasoline. In the late 1970s the Brazilians developed a car engine to run on alcohol. The alcohol is made by **distilling** sugar, which is one reason why Brazil produces such a large amount of sugarcane.

Journeys that could take days can be made in hours by plane. There are hundreds of small airports, even deep in the Amazon Basin, as well as several modern international airports.

In the last century railroads were built to serve the mining areas of southeast Brazil. However, the routes have never been expanded, and today the lines are used mainly for **freight**. Most goods go by road except in the Amazon Basin, where the rivers are in constant use. Ocean-going ships can sail from the Atlantic, 1,000 mi (1,600 km) up to Manaus and on into Peru.

20 Government and economy

The Congress building in Brasilia. The dome on the left is the Senate and the bowl on the right is the Chamber of Deputies.

After the fall of the military government in 1985, Brazil returned to a **democratic government** with elections. Brazil is a federal republic, similar to that of the United States.

The head of the country is the President, who holds office for five years. Congress, which makes laws and policies for Brazil as a whole, is split into two; the Senate and Chamber of Deputies.

Brazil has twenty-six states plus the Federal District of Brasilia. Each of these elects three senators and a number of deputies to Congress. The states can also make their own laws to a certain extent. In each state the Legislative Assembly is elected to do this and an elected governor is in overall charge.

Brazil is just beginning to experience democracy after years of military rule during which there was little political freedom. There are now many political parties. Although Brazil has returned to democracy, power and control has stayed with the wealthy families and large companies, much as it did before.

President Collor, who was elected in 1989, faces some serious economic problems. High inflation is one of the worst. At one point it was 1,000 percent per year – which means that an ice-cream costing 100 Cruzeiros in January would cost 1,100 Cruzeiros by the following December! The other problem is the massive 120 billion dollar debt. Over the last thirty-five years, the country has borrowed huge sums of money from abroad to pay for projects like the Trans-Amazonian Highway, hydroelectric dams and big mining and industrial ventures. Brazil does not have the money to pay back such a big debt, and foreign organizations are working with the Brazilian government to try to find a solution.

Above Because inflation is so high, the money in Brazil often changes. The 100, 200 and 500 notes have been overstamped saying they are now Cruzeiros (and no longer Cruzados Novos).

Right Local police stand to attention at a parade in Belem.

Facing the future

There are two Brazils: one is a twenty-first century land of opportunity; the other is backward, poor and struggling to survive. Not only is there this contrast between the rich and the poor all over Brazil, but there are also similar contrasts between the regions. Rapid population growth and the movement of people to the *favelas* of the cities are adding to this problem. How to even out the wealth in Brazil is one of the main issues facing the country in the future.

Life for the poor in Brazil can mean living and begging on the streets.

Left Huge areas of forest have been cleared to build roads through remote parts of Brazil.

Below Brazilian children attending a special day set aside to teach them about the Amerindians of the Amazon.

Brazil has severe economic difficulties, with high inflation and a massive foreign debt to pay back. Exploiting Brazil's many natural resources is one way to create growth and help the economy. There are consequently great pressures to develop the many unused resources of the Amazon – for farming, for hydro-electric power and for minerals. What many Brazilians see as progress, **ecologists** see as destruction. As yet, it is not clear what the effects of the loss of the rainforests will be or how they could be used for the long-term benefit of Brazil. If the rainforest is destroyed, Brazil is likely to lose its greatest future **asset**. The rights of the Amerindians to their land and way of life is another issue that still needs to be resolved.

Brazil has a good climate, plenty of land and huge natural resources. If some of the economic and social problems facing the country can be overcome, Brazil can begin to use its many natural advantages in a long-term way that will benefit all its population. It is already the leading South American country and has the potential to be one of the richest countries in the world.

Glossary

Abolition   Putting an end to something.
Amerindians   The people who inhabited South America before the arrival of Europeans. The Europeans called the people "Indians" because, when they arrived in Brazil, they did not realize they were in a new (American) continent and believed they were in the East Indies.
Ancestors   People in a family who are no longer alive, such as great-grandparents and their parents and grandparents.
Asset   Something worth having.
Bauxite   A clay from which aluminum comes.
Civilian   Not belonging to the armed forces.
Colonial period   A time when people from another country govern a territory – here it means when the Portuguese ruled Brazil.
Canopy   The mass of branches and leaves at the tops of the trees in a forest.
Cults   Kinds of religious beliefs.
Debt   Something owed to somebody else, often money.
Democratic government   A government chosen by the people.
Distilling   The process by which alcohol is made.
Drought-ridden   Suffering from long periods without rain.
Ecologists   People who study the environment.
Economy   The careful management of resources to avoid unnecessary expense or waste; activities dealing with the production, distribution and use of goods and services.
Ecosystem   A community of plants and animals and the environment in which they live.
Equatorial   Of or near the equator.
Escarpment   A steep slope.
Exploit   To take advantage of something or to make use of something.

Extinction   When a species of plant or animal dies out completely.
First Grade   In Brazil, the first eight years of school.
Free Trade Zone   An area where there are no taxes on goods. Manaus was made a Free Trade Zone in 1966 to help boost the economy of this Amazonian city.
Freight   Goods or cargo (not people) that are transported from one place to another.
Hydroelectric   Producing electricity by using water power.
Illiterate   Unable to read or write.
Immigrants   People who come to live in a country from elsewhere.
Infertile   Not able to produce good crops.
Inflation   Price rises due to increase in the amount of money in circulation.
Lianas   Climbing woody plants that look a bit like rope.
Machete   A kind of heavy knife.
Malaria   A disease caused by the bite of a mosquito that lives in hot, swampy areas.
Malnutrition   Poor health caused by lack of nourishment, usually as a result of not having enough to eat or an unbalanced diet.
Mammal   An animal that is warm-blooded and has hair or fur. Mammals give birth to live young, which they feed with their own milk.
Missionaries   Members of religious groups who go to a foreign country to carry out religious, social or medical work.
Monarchy   A nation with a king or queen as head of state.
Primary rainforest   The original forest that is mostly untouched.
Racially tolerant   Accepting, and living peacefully with, people of a different color or race.
Republic   A country without a king, queen or emperor but which instead has an elected leader such as a president.

Roman Catholicism The part of the Christian Church that has the Pope as its head.

Sap Juice from a tree.

Second Grade In Brazil, the three years of secondary school from age 16 to age 18.

Slaves People who are forced to work for others, usually without being paid.

Southern hemisphere The part of the world south of the equator.

Species A group of animals or plants that are similar.

Staple The main part of a diet; the most important food or crop.

Tableland A flat, but high, area of land; a plateau.

Tributaries Rivers that flow into another, larger river.

Books to read

Bender, Evelyn. *Brazil*. New York: Chelsea House, 1989.

Carpenter, Mark. *Brazil: An Awakening Giant*. Minneapolis: Dillon, 1987.

Cross, Wilbur. *Brazil*. Chicago: Children's Press, 1984.

Haverstock, Nathan A. *Brazil in Pictures*. Minneapolis: Lerner Publications, 1987.

Picture acknowledgments
All photographs were taken by Julia Waterlow with the exception of the following: Bruce Coleman Ltd 8 (top); Sue Cunningham *cover*, 16, 17, 31, 33 (below); South American Pictures 9 (top left/Tony Morrison), 12. The maps were supplied by Peter Bull.

Index